Whispers To The Oblivion

Shreyashree Sarkar

BookLeaf Publishing

Presentation by *BookLeaf Publishing*

Web: www.bookleafpub.com

E-mail: info@bookleafpub.com

ISBN: 9789357615556

First edition 2023

To all those who loved me, and all those who didn't

It's you who has made me, me.

ACKNOWLEDGEMENT

I am deeply indebted to Bookleaf Publishers for debuting me as a poet. My sincere acknowledgments for the hard work of my editors and book cover designer. I would also like to thank my family and friends for always inspiring me to write.

PREFACE

When the passion in my veins
becomes the poison in my blood,
and death comes closer by a step,
I will not shrivel in sudden fear
or dissolve into a mist of a pitiable plight
For even when I die,
My words will illuminate lives with it's
perennial light.

~ a melancholic poet

Of Love

Ruby Sunsets

I saw
The burden of a dragonfly
Lift its wings in air,
In sheer elation, or despair?

The burden of dragonfly
Of ruby sunsets through flecks of leaves
In sheer elation or despair
Silhouettes of blurry words against the corpse of
a silent city

Of ruby sunsets through flecks of leaves
I saw his eyes shimmer like diamonds
Silhouettes of blurry words against the corpse of
a silent city
Slipped into our blind tunnels of memory

I saw his eyes shimmer like diamonds
Then in a tide came those words
Slipped into our blind tunnels of memory
And sprouted in rubbles of hope
Our phoenix love.

Autumn

The melody onto your chest that plays,
Muddy rains on the window as the evening
slays.
Your voice echo to the tune of my labored breath
And aside, on the floor, our masks layeth
You show your scars and corpses from the past
I lay my fears to rest at last
My body, you worship in your lover's grace
Holy rituals in our sweet embrace
Goosebumps like vales on my forlorn skin
Awakened spirits like embers within
Amidst our rubbles, blows an ignorant breeze,
My soul so long a slave, you set to release.

Nirvana

In me, you'll find the calm
you'd been searching in the vast tumults of life,
the yearnings of a nightingale
bereaved, bereft of love.

In me, you'll find the soul that fits
into the crevices of yours like puzzle pieces,
and the aurora your midnights die into.

In me, my love, you'll find the woman,
complete like a blossom in spring.

In me, your nirvana.

Glitter

4

The moment he held me, I knew,
like an undaunted blossom amidst the thorns,
a new love grew.
Mosaics of thoughts stitched together,
hands entwined, whispers made promises of
'forever'
visionaries of stars, galaxies, and sunshine,
glitter in his eyes reflected behind mine.

A Moment

This moment of love,
deafeningly silent between our lips
The rift in our beds,
merging with the bridge of your body.
You, in excruciating pain
as I apologize
midway between a logical exchange.
Your inability to tether emotions,
lead you to shed down rivers
and then you come snuggling closer
onto my lap,
touching the moment
with quivering lips and gawky fingers :

A moment of melancholy.

Your heavy breath on my skin,
speaks volumes as you keep mum.
It jitters me off thoughts, the howling of curfew
signals.
Shutters closing outside
and then the closing of your eyelids :

A moment of overwhelm

Another tear, you couldn't hold in,
as coffee cups lay aside in dismay
I blinked and it passed :

A moment of pity.

Then rushed a moment of relief,
as you take my hands again.
You forgive me. It took you only a moment?

Only a moment of love?

How?

How do you do that?
Undress me one layer at a time,
and kiss that void deep into
the pits of my stomach with those eyes?

And how do you tangle and detangle
locked away abysses of passion in me
effortlessly, like strands of hair
snarled in your fingers

How do you fit with ease,
into my arms like puzzle pieces?
We were strangers,
after all.

New Dawn

Beneath foggy blankets,
we lay in the still darkness,
discovering hands on hands
and heartbeats on heartbeats.

Touching the edge of our lips
is ecstasy - an unforgotten craving
But caught in limbo, our words turn defiant
and skin to skin our goosebumps hum.

Is it just mouths, or are we one?
At dawn, like the moonlight
plunging into the embrace of the sun...

Losing you

How do I tell you that fear shudders through me still,
even when you clasp me in your arms so tight?
Like a shadow lurks around, oblivious to our sight.
A silence prevails before the storm;
that blanches my soul when you are gone
So I sit there clutching my loneliness closer,
to fill the void he left within
And picture my past: shades of gray in a canvas of grime
For I can never let go of what I dread,
Losing you as I lost him.

Aquamarine

The way your eyes smirk at my existence
and heavy breaths sublime under hallucinating
lights
The rifts of your wet lips, abhorrent and
unawaiting
On mine sometimes, sometimes gone
A lover's sigh, and poet's respite,

You.

The splash of aquamarine
to my gloomy canvas of life.

Of Heartaches

Freckle

I was a virgin canvas,
your lips couldn't stain.

I had waterfalls inside my chest,
your eyes couldn't contain.

I ached in places
your hands couldn't touch,

I spoke of beauty
words couldn't adorn much.

So what you loved that beauty spot
on the edge of my waist,
Alongside thrived a freckle
you had already abandoned in haste.

My Doomsday Bell

I came back from the bridge bathed in tears,
ugly with the torments over all these years.
Verses fluttered on my lips like a solitary dove,
only to drown the broken bones into a fresh,
dangerous love.
Wallowing in the aura of his wintry gaze
never knew what magic put my soul in such a
daze.
Does he read me? For I'm afraid,
of the age-old prophecies, bards have made.
Crippled in the succor of his treacherous spell,
there, tolls my doomsday bell.

Of Melancholia

Escape

With her dreams cradled on my eyelids,
sleepless nights have been spent.
With her crooning, I held inward,
a sober whiskey drained.
Between sonnets to her eyes,
and musings of her touch,
the heart had been defiant on evenings
I had seen too much.
Of shadows I quest,
and dreams devour,
My heart races through the night
And love lulls me to a soothing shore.

I wake under the sultry sun
burning me to rust
And then, I find myself running again
For escape, I must.

Shipwreck

What are you, but a stranger now?

A chest of secrets held too long,
The no-man's land between my right and wrong
A letter of love from April nine,
Cells I craved with each of mine.

What am I, but a shipwreck
in the storms of your love.

Wilted Flowers Never Bloom

Tonight, my heart feels like this:
A crumpled note of love thrown over the abyss...
That lost and damned one didn't know,
of thorns, that, with roses grow.
And my heart, a fool, fell again,
for the trap that love had lain
So suffer, suffer till its doom,
Darling, wilted flowers never bloom.

Graves of Pain

She, alike the oceans
concealed in her chest.
All the horror that passed through her,
disasters put to rest.

She alike the fiery lava,
charring self to dust.
Amidst the grip of blurry fear,
and follies of her past.

She, alike the leaves of fall,
swerving her way to doom.
Faded amongst a thousand shades,
where dreary silhouettes loom.

She, alike the winter bird,
a herald to storms and rain.
Chirping in the waning light,
Her nest on graves of pain.

Deep Cut

One December evening,
preceding supper,
the knife had taken
too much of my flesh.
I couldn't help losing dexterity
on my culinary skills,
And then on all of my life,
one crimson drop at a time.

The kind doctor
had covered my wounds,
promised it would heal.
And as I lay
at night aching every place
I wondered who'd bandage
my bleeding heart,
Who'd promise if it will heal?

Life is

Life is, but snow.
crumbling down
as I try to hold on
firm in fistfuls.

And I stare out of my window
with blurry eyes
shortening breaths,
as if it were winter days
of Iowa City.

The sun shining upon the snow
a blazing white light
blinding when it hits the eyes
I wish everything
came to a standstill
like the white frosting on trees
I wish the struggle were over
One day,
Today
at mid-noon?
in the evening?
Life moves forth,
time passes by.
Pain remains

Stubborn.
Resilient.

I have to shovel
the heaviness in my heart
I have to dissolve the knots
in the pits of my stomach.
Please, God, give me the strength
to be able to breathe
in the next moment.

Black

Black is not a color.

Black is the awry trajectory
to home every night,
the hues of cut-throat
emotions at 3 a.m.

No, not the little dress you wore
at your 18th birthday party,
Black is tearing down the walls,
howling and crying afterward
because the bullies are your friends.

Black are the corners
you sit and slit.
You bleed from everywhere and
smell of a sweet release.

Black is the reverberating voice
of a bygone lover that
doesn't let you sleep.
Of days you live in a crowd
and wonder why
do you feel so hauntingly alone?

Black is not a color
Black is the absence of any color.

Ghosts of the Past

Awake from slumber,
still in a trance,
my being liquidating
into droplets,
one after the other
dripping like the rain
from the heavens.

Black demons,
ugly demons,
ugly memories
from the past
that I revisit
tirelessly again.
History repeats itself
and I break apart,

What do I do with
this lump in my throat
this lovesickness
this homesickness
this congestion
in my chest?

Touch is such
a lovely feeling
but what if
it had an evil side,
an overlooked
premonition?

Love is such
a homely feeling
but what if
I told you today
that it can too,
set fire to all things
you've called home-
people, places, and time?

Inferno

It's only now that I realize,
decades of mourning will cease no cries.

Love and disaster sewed in one,
the eternal inferno I was destined to burn.

Damaged was I, maybe a little more now?
revived regrets into piles, and how!

Like dead petunias on the sea afloat,
like the blandness of a solitary piano note,

I fell apart from the world to endure,
The burden of a soul, impure.